You're So Sweet

PHILADELPHIA

We were such V-I-PEEPS
that time we

_____

You are some-bunny
very special because

_____

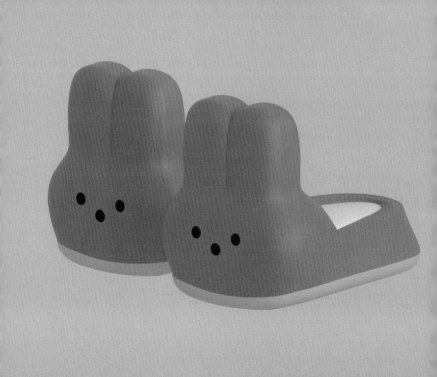

You make me feel all warm
and fuzzy when you

_____

All our PEEPS® say that
we're the best of buds because

_____

Nothing's sweeter than the way you

_____

You're the most

_____

person I've ever known.

We can conquer any challenge
together so long as we

_____

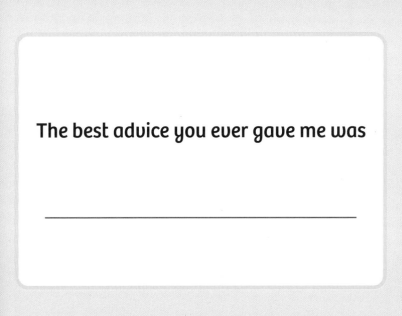

The best advice you ever gave me was

_____

If someone named a holiday after you,
it would be called

_____

_____

was the best gift you ever gave me.

We were two of the biggest party
PEEPS® that time we

_____

If our friendship were a movie,
it would be about

_____

If I could borrow one talent from you, I'd choose your

_____

I've never laughed harder
than that time we

_____

The one thing we have most
in common is our

_____

You were one tough Chick
that time you

_____

If you have a bad hair day,
I'd cheer you up by

_____

I wouldn't trade your love
and friendship for

_____

We lived our best PEEPS®
life that time we

_____

If I could relive just one of our adventures, it would be

_____

One of these days we should finally get around to

_____

We were two cool PEEPS®
that time we

_____

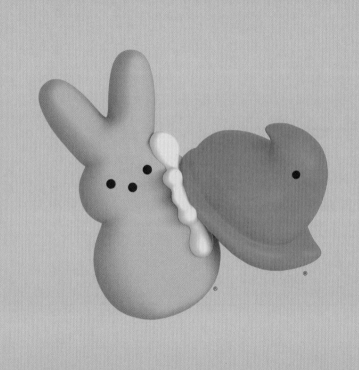

We stick together like

_____

and

_____

If our friendship were a pop song,
it would be

_____

You look super fleek when you wear

_____

Some would call what we have
a friendship, but I prefer to call it

_____

_____

is definitely our favorite
guilty pleasure.

You're one special Chick because

_____

If I had a time machine,
I'd revisit that moment when we

_____

Nothing lightens my mood like your

_____

I love to watch you

_____

Our favorite dish
is an extra helping of

_____

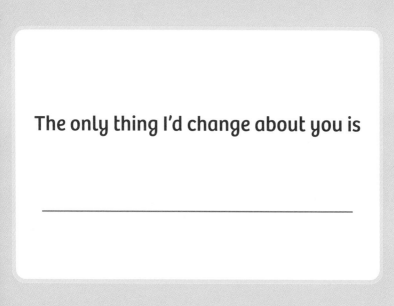

The only thing I'd change about you is

_____

_____

was the craziest thing
we ever did together.

_____

will always be our "special place."

I knew you weren't
the average PEEPS® when you

_____

There's only one thing I love
more than you and that's

_____

We should take a road trip to

_____

Your

_____

cheers me up instantly.

Our deepest, most profound
conversations are usually about

_____

We go together like PEEPS®
of a feather when we

_____

Our perfect night would be

_____

You helped me learn to

_____

The most embarrassing thing
we ever did together was

_____

If I had to sum up our friendship
in one word, it would be

_____

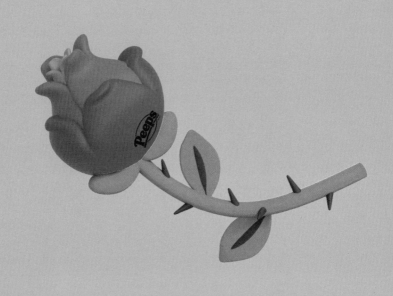

No matter what our friendship holds,
I vow to always

_____

We go together like
two PEEPS® in a pod.

RP Studio™
Hachette Book Group
1290 Avenue of the Americas, New York, NY 10104
www.runningpress.com
@Running_Press

First Edition: January 2025

Published by RP Studio, an imprint of Hachette Book Group, Inc.
The RP Studio name and logo are trademarks of Hachette Book Group, Inc.

Running Press books may be purchased in bulk for business, educational, or promotional use. For more information, please contact your local bookseller or the Hachette Book Group Special Markets Department at Special.Markets@hbgusa.com.

The publisher is not responsible for websites (or their content) that are not owned by the publisher.

Written by Sam Stall

Design by Tanvi Baghele

Illustrations by Melissa Mathieson

ISBN: 978-0-7624-8841-4

Printed in China

1010

10 9 8 7 6 5 4 3 2 1